Daydreaming...

a collection of random thoughts, hopes, and fears

Toluwani Tiphany

BookLeaf
Publishing

India | USA | UK

Presentation by *BookLeaf Publishing*

Web: www.bookleafpub.com

E-mail: info@bookleafpub.com

ISBN: 9789358361339

First edition 2022

Dedicated to Winnie Oriakhi.

Rest well Mumzy.

ACKNOWLEDGEMENT

There is no amount of gratitude that would be enough to thank my darling Mumzy. The first person to truly see me as worthwhile. Thank you for showing me how it feels to be loved and cherished. I also thank you for making me do all those writing exercises as a kid. You always saw potential in me, especially when I couldn't see it in myself. I'm taking your word for it and will try my best to continue to learn and grow. I love you, I miss you and I hope you are finally resting well.

To all my friends and family who have been there for me during these hard times, thank you. You are a constant reminder that there is still good in this world. I hope this serves as a nice surprise for you all.

PREFACE

Honestly, it is a miracle that this book even exists. I have always had a love-hate relationship with writing, even when I realised it was something I very much wanted to pursue. I find that with many art forms there seems to be this struggle, this stress, that one must experience to produce a piece of work, or performance. Personally, I think it comes from a sincere desire for perfection. Which isn't wrong - it means you care. However, my method of caring has often resulted in me never finishing the work, or sometimes not even starting it...

It is so much easier to just picture it in my head, where it is perfect and I can save myself the heartbreak of never being satisfied.

This is a thought process that I have and still am working hard on changing. With my Mum's encouragement and advice, I was making progress until –

My worst nightmare happened.

Sadly, my Mum passed away back in 2019. I cannot begin to describe how world shattering that was and still is. There are still days I wake up and think I'm in an alternate timeline. Needless to say, her passing changed a lot of things. One of those was my writing. I just couldn't and wouldn't write. It was too much, too soon, and anything I did write for school purposes felt like I was yanking a tooth out.

That's why I see this book as a breakthrough for me. My work may not be perfect, it may not be as rich and as colourful as I had imagined it. But it is what I've written...and completed. This is something I can always look back on, when I think I'm not capable, when I forget that we all have to start from somewhere before we can move forward.

Through this book I have taken baby steps back into accepting my feelings. Filled with desires, concerns and narratives that have randomly crossed my mind. I hope to expand more on my writing and creative journey in the future and do my Mum proud.

To anyone grieving the loss of a loved one - I am sincerely sorry and pray you receive the comfort you need. I don't believe loss is something that can ever be 'fixed'. As time goes by you learn to live with it. You learn to remember them in laughter and in tears. You come to understand that the pain will never go away, because you loved them. Perhaps like me there are things you find difficult to do because of your loss. Everyone's experience is different, but I hope this book serves as proof that there is still a life to be lived, and memories to be made.

My heart is with you. Please be kind to yourself, and take things one day at a time. God bless,

Toluwani Tiphany

1. Pink Purple Blue

Pink, Purple, Blue

They're all inside of you.

All inside of me?

Yes, who else would it be?

Blue is calm, blue is chill

And cares not for turbulent thrills.

Purple is strong, wise and old

Her rich elegance always bold.

Pink is sweet, loving and pure

Harm not her heart

That's for sure.

But hide not her tears or her pain

Through scorching droughts or heavy rain.

For what you feel inside is human too.

It's Pink, it's Purple, and it's Blue.

2. Touch The Sky

Touch the sky

Touch the stars

Touch the world with all your heart.

With all your strength, will and might

Let them all see such a sight!

Spread your wings and fly up high

Let the universe be your guide

Let the wind be your horse

As you journey beyond the earth.

And when all is done and said,

Let the clouds be your bed.

3. The Start of Summer

Ahhh.

A delicate smile eases onto my face as I'm greeted by a gust of wind.

The sun kisses my cheeks and the clouds yield to miles of blue.

Could this be the miracle I've been waiting for?

My nose tingles with the fresh scent of the ocean.

Step by step…

I have brought myself to the beach.

I gaze upon the ocean's rhythmic beauty as silver glitter flutters on her surface.

I feel the weight of my chest lift, as another breeze carries me away cooling the sun's passionate affection.

Finally, she has come.

With the end of May and the start of June

Summer has come to end my gloom.

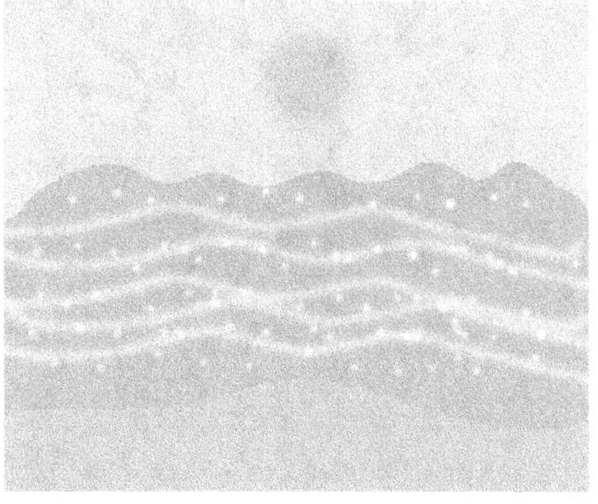

4. To Fall in Love

To fall in love is to drown in the sweet
syrup of the maple tree

To suffocate under the pillowy feathers of a
dove

And to choke on the ripe flesh of a succulent
peach

To fall in love is to willingly die again and
again, in pure pure bliss.

5. Love is a Creature

Love is a creature

Of pain and sorrow

Of joy and healing.

It lurks in the heart, begging to be fed.

Begging to be seen, to be felt.

Immortal, it survives suppression,
repression and oppression.

Its passion blooms and thrives, even in
poison.

Constructive and Destructive.

To be feared and to be craved.

Love is a creature

I dare not tame.

6. Irrational Foam

Why?

Why must I feel this?

This tingling and prickling of an intrusive glow.

It bubbles and froths up as an irrational foam.

Invisible to the eye yet seen by all.

I can't hide it.

Do I…want to hide it?

I detest it! Despise it!

Yet I fear its departure.

I fear *your* departure.

Because each time I see you, hear you or think of you

This tingling and prickling intrusive glow bubbles ferociously froths aggressively into an inexplicable completely irrational foam.

7. Nothing

I sat here waiting for a dream,

But the dream never came to me.

I sat there waiting for a spark,

But the ignition had stopped working.

I looked up and prayed for a sign,

But my request was declined.

I looked down and said don't you dare…and
left them with a heart gripping stare.

I turned left, right and all around but
still…nothing.

Nothing… nothing.

Until that nothing was something…

It was this.

8. If I was a Flower

If I was a flower, would I die

a hundred, thousand, million times?

Picked and plucked, trimmed and cut

as per your desire?

If I was a flower, would I be

the enchanting mistress of the honey bees?

If I was a flower, would I live

as the rose of all roses,

or the weed of all weeds?

Blossoming in praise, nurtured and kept

or shrivelling in poison, pulled and yanked?

If I was a flower, would I die

a hundred, thousand, million times?

9. Please Don't Hate Me

Please don't hate me

for I can't see

all the love you have for me

Please don't hate me

for I can't hear

the sincere wishes you whisper in my ear

Please don't hate me

for I can't smell

the scent of hope in which you dwell

Please don't hate me

for I can't taste

the sweet words that have turned into waste

Please don't hate me

for I can't touch

the trust of your hands…it's not enough

10.   Princess Night

Ebony skin

Raven hair

Indigo eyes

The one and only Princess night.

With crystals draping her from head to toe

And deep garments which under flow.

A quiet smile

And a harmless sigh

Friend of the moon

Friend of the stars

With a raise of her hand, her dreams are
ours.

11.   The Pink Bride – Intrusion

As the wind drifts past my ear

And my feet become lead

The clouds draw darker in my head

Neither the sun's parting glow

Nor the sea's twinkling streams

Can lift my head up from this deep

But a glance of pink on the sand

Brings my thoughts to a stand

Whether in awe or jealous desire

I watch a bride in pink attire.

12.   The Pink Bride – Delusion

I stand here, in absolute awe, as she absorbs the sunset.

Veiled in glittering shades of rose, toes dipped in the sea, she is curled by the edge.

The wind boldly lifts a layer and finally, I see her face.

Jewels play in her dense curls, like stars at midnight.

Flower dust shimmers on her mocha skin.

Her morganite eyes glisten with pools of…grief?

She turns to me and smiles, as a single stream glides down her cheek.

I find myself floating towards her as my own pools begin to form.

I close my eyes to wipe them away and a sweet scent blows past me.

When I open my eyes…she is nowhere to be seen.

13.   The Pink Bride – Confusion

What was now?

What would I be?

My tears run cold

And my body flies free

No sense of sight

But I see it all,

I feel it all

Hear it

Smell it

Taste it all

What is it?

What is this?

I remember everything but know nothing at
all!

The clouds have cleared

My mind has sight

But where is the Pink Bride?

Who is the Pink Bride?

 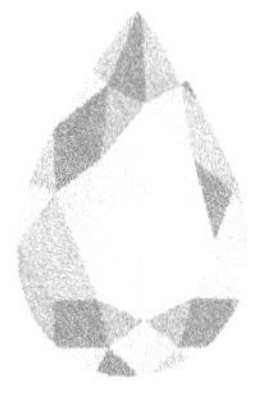 

14.   Thoughts

I lie awake – poisoned by my own thoughts

I lie awake – healed by my own thoughts

I toss and turn – struggling with my own
thoughts

I shed a tear – saddened by my own
thoughts

I cry for help – and I am answered by my
own thoughts

I run away – but I am captured by my own
thoughts.

15. At Season's Bend

Murky hangs the sky

Bitter flows the wind

As day dawns

And season bends

The Sun's mercy trickles away

And the buttery light that once kissed my face

Is faded by Autumn's sincere embrace

16.   Why does the Mermaid?

Why does the mermaid hate her own tail?

Why does she despise her iridescent scales?

Why does she wish to be upon the land,

when she could so easily die at man's hand?

Why does her beauty cause her to cry,

tempting her to gore out her eyes?

Why does she always look up and pray,

that drowning in water will end her day?

What did she hear, what did she see?

What made her feel all these horrible
things?

Why does the mermaid hate her own tail?

Why does she despise her iridescent scales?

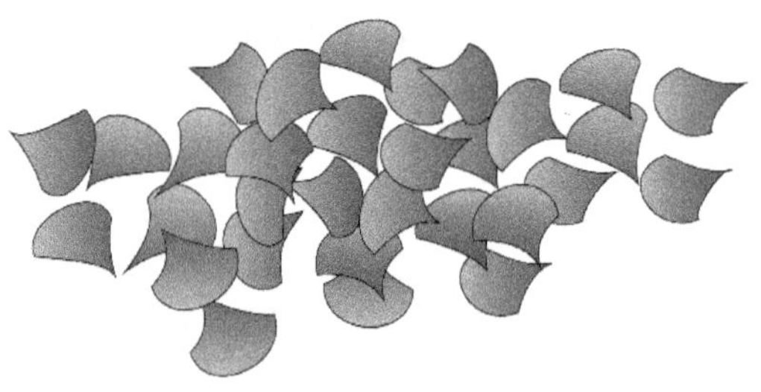

17.   How the Goddess Died

How did the goddess die?

You dare ask?

You truly dare ask?

When you begged at her feet

Tugged at her hair

Demanding her to help you

Requiring her to save you

Regardless of the price.

Her mane shed and her skin cracked.

Her mind broke and her heart wept.

All to build the world you wished to see!

Perhaps she is to blame.

For the size of her heart

Was too big and too full

To witness your hurt.

But when she was hurting…

What did you do?

You tilted your head

And wondered how she bled.

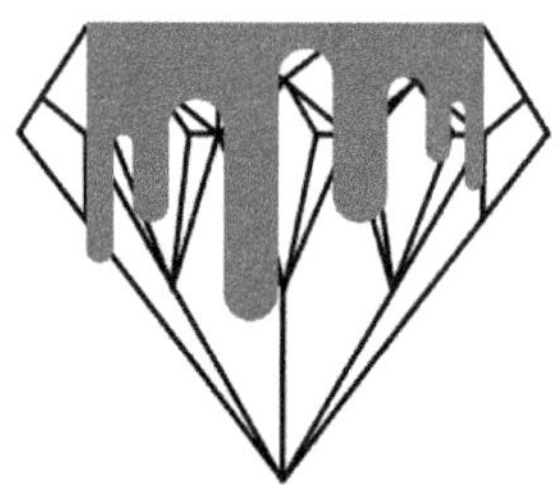

18.   Everything's ok

Everything's ok

Everything's just fine

I've added another year

And I'm ageing like fine wine

Though you're no longer here

My heart remains the same

With sweet memories of all the love you
ever gave

I try to be ok because everything's ok

Yet the tears betray my calm like they're
creating another storm

Some days I forget, forget that you're gone,

Then suddenly I remember as if I never
knew before

I don't know what to do, I don't know what
to say

The nightmare repeats and I'm no longer
the same

How did I get here, how has it been years?

And why am I still here

When you're no longer near?

19.   The Little Things

It's the little things that prick my toes

pluck my hairs and peck my nose

It's the little things that make me sigh

sting my eyes and make me cry

It's the little things that build and build

an avalanche against my shield

Yet it's the little things here and there

that show me when someone cares

It's the big things that started small

little by little they all grew tall

A good deed here and a good deed there

it's the little things we all can share

20.   The Next Step

I sit and stare deep into the empty air

Heart full to the brim of dreams

Yet engulfed in fear of what could be

Scared to lose

Excited to

Yet

So

So

I ofte

And finally   o take

www.ingramcontent.com/pod-product-compliance
Lightning Source LLC
LaVergne TN
LVHW021310200726
843509LV00012B/1862